Burnt Cookies

Burnt Cookies

and other devos for girls on the go

Lois Walfrid Johnson

Standard Publishing
cincinnati, ohio

❀

To Jessica and Jennifer,
Karin and Elise,
with love from
our awesome Master Baker
and from me

❀

Contents

Dear Girlfriend,

Are you the cookie baker at your house? Isn't it fun to put together those good ingredients? And doesn't that dough taste yummy? Maybe you have a brother or sister who snitches it from you, or maybe you're like many kids—you love to gobble the dough before it's baked.

If there's anything left after the snitchers have a taste, you slide a pan with neat mountains of dough into the oven. Soon the scent of baking fills your house. When you pop the cookies out on a cooling rack, you've created a treat for yourself, your friends, and your family.

But sometimes things don't turn out that well. You begin surfing the net or talking on the phone and forget all about the cookies. The inviting scent of baking vanishes in the smell of burnt cookies.

Sometimes our lives are like that. What starts out looking good changes in one split second. Where we had hope, we feel out of sorts, disappointed, upset, or angry. Things didn't turn out the way we wanted them to. In those times life seems like a burnt cookie—scorched on the bottom or dark and dried to a crisp all the way through.

But guess what? All of us have the opportunity to discover something. Could it be that even on burnt cookie days, there's a Master Baker hanging out in the kitchen?

His name is Jesus. Every one of us can ask him for help. Best of all, he loves us the way we are and wants to encourage us too.

So let's find out more, OK? Let's talk the way we would with a special girlfriend. Maybe our burnt cookies will turn into something good!

Dear Girlfriend,

You know what? There's something I'm starting to figure out. Lots of times I'm scared—really scared—that I won't be able to do something, like give a speech. Do you feel that way too? Maybe all of us have fears. Some of them may seem unlikely to happen, but most of the time they feel real! Will I pass this test? Will I make the team? What will I be when I grow up? Sometimes fear stops me dead in my tracks, and I am unable to move. Or it keeps me awake at night, feeling frightened and alone. That is, if I let it. But God has a secret weapon we can use to send our fears into outer space. . . .

Fear Factor

❦ Recipe du Jour ❦

"I feel like my life has been full of firsts and unknowns," said Courtney.

She named some of them. Starting middle school. Baby-sitting for the first time. Giving a speech in front of her class. Most of us can relate. We've been in similar situations and have probably had the symptoms that go along with them—butterflies in our stomach, "cotton" mouth, and clammy hands.

Sometimes it's just common sense not to try something new—like when people are trying to pressure us into doing something that we shouldn't. But at other times, fear gets in the way of our trying good things, even simple things. We hold back because we wonder, *What's going to happen? What if others laugh at me?*

At times even little kids experience these fears. Kevin didn't want to get dressed for preschool one morning. "I don't want to go," he told his mom and pulled the covers over his head.

"Why not?" she asked. "You've been having so much fun there."

"I'm not going anymore," he said.

"OK, but can you tell me why?"

"Because," Kevin answered.

Every morning they had the same conversation when it was time to get up for school, and Kevin always answered, "Because."

"What's wrong?" his mother kept asking. "Why won't you tell me?"

Then one day tears welled up in Kevin's blue eyes. "They want me to skip," he said. "And I don't know how!"

"To skip? I'm sure they don't expect you to do that. You're too young."

But Kevin kept insisting, and that night he held his mom's hand while the two of them skipped around and around in big circles. It took Kevin awhile, but he finally managed to stay on one foot. The next day his mom checked with his teacher.

"No, we don't expect the children to know how to skip," she said. "We just asked them to try."

Because we're older, the fear of a 4-year-old not being able to skip sounds a bit silly. But sometimes fear starts when

> Trying to avoid a situation might work for a while, but the fear is still there.

> What's going to happen? What if others laugh at me?

we're very young. If we don't face those fears, they might set limits on our future.

"I want to do well," said Sarah, "but I'm afraid to try something new. What if I'm not good at it? What if I fall on my face in front of the other kids? What if they all laugh at me?"

Sometimes fear starts when we're very young. If we don't face those fears, they might set limits on our future.

Most of the time when we're faced with fear-producing situations, all that anybody expects from us is our willingness to try.

"For a long time, my fear of new things kept me from trying," Courtney explained. "For me, every little hill was becoming a huge mountain."

Trying to avoid a situation might work for a while, but the fear is still there. Fear that needs to be conquered makes us uneasy. But what happens if we face up to our fears? We can tell ourselves, *OK, I don't know how I'll do, but I'll try because that's better than doing nothing.*

"What it really means is focusing on my goal instead of on my fear," says Erika. "When I give a speech, I think about what I want to say. I focus on how I can help people instead of on my wobbly knees."

And don't forget this—as a member of God's family, we never have to face anything alone. It helps to talk about our fear with a person who will understand. That person can help us know whether or not a fear is real and how to put it in perspective.

Burnt Cookies

Best of all, whenever we face fears and feel inadequate, we can tell God about them. We can be honest: "I'm scared about giving a speech (or whatever it is). What do you want me to know?" We can ask him to give us a thought or a Bible verse to hang onto. With his help we'll accomplish far more than if we try to tackle our fears alone. Like Erika, we might even surprise ourselves.

As a member of God's family, we never have to face anything alone.

"Another one of those firsts was trying out for a special choir," she said. "But I knew that God was with me, so I wasn't quite as scared. I was sure my voice would squeak. But guess what? When I repeated Philippians 4:13 to myself, God helped me go beyond my fear. I made the choir!"

❁ Main Ingredient ❁

"I can do everything with the help of Christ who gives me the strength I need." Philippians 4:13 *(NLT)*

❁ Temperature Control ❁

Lord, please help me to face my fears and deal with them. Show me how to go beyond my fear when it involves something good I need to learn. Make me willing to try the things that will help me grow into a better person.

Dear Girlfriend,

Do you ever wish that you could be someone else? Sometimes I just want to look like the other girls and do the same things they do. Wouldn't it be great to be the prettiest girl in class or the most creative artist in school? But do you suppose God can use even the things I don't like about myself? He's given me special abilities too! But sometimes it takes a long time to figure out what those special things are. . . .

Target Practice

❀ Recipe du Jour ❀

Christa hadn't seen the elderly woman for several days. But her words were still ringing in Christa's ears.

"My, but you've gotten tall!" the woman had said. "You must be the tallest girl in your class!"

Tallest! Tallest! Tallest! Christa thought bitterly. *Why remind me?*

If only she could scrunch down into a tiny creature, she'd head for the nearest mouse hole. Then no one would see how different she was from everyone else.

Sometimes when we feel different from other kids, we're able to do something about it. For instance, no one likes to be caught wearing a skirt when everyone else is in jeans. Yet there are other things that aren't so easy to change. Is there a way we can learn to live with them?

Burnt Cookies

Right now we might be growing faster than other kids. Take the boy who lives down the street. Even though he's our age, he hasn't even started to get his height. It's hard to remember that boys often have their growth spurt later than girls.

> Sometimes what bothers us most are things that other people don't even notice.

Or we may have the opposite problem.

"Short stuff—that's me. I hate my nickname," said one girl who was shorter than all of her friends. But what she really hated was the way she felt about herself when she heard that name.

Instead of being too tall or too short, we might feel we're too fat or too thin. We might have skin problems, braces on our teeth, or be developing later than other girls.

The list of all the things we feel are wrong can be endless. And we haven't even touched on the serious challenges that people face every day!

Sometimes what bothers us most are things that other people don't even notice. Yet they seem so big to us that we can't see beyond them.

"When I keep looking at my weaknesses, that's all I see," said Jasmine. "It's like I've turned myself into a great big target—a bull's-eye for archery practice. I keep shooting arrows at myself. And it's not much fun feeling those arrows strike. They hurt. And every one of those arrows tells me, "There's something wrong with you!"

But do you know what's really wrong? We compare ourselves to others. We take what we see as something weak about ourselves and compare it to someone else's strength. No wonder we feel we're no good!

Jasmine discovered something. *I can choose to stop the target practice and look at God's promises instead!*

God accepts us as we are. When we don't like ourselves we're saying, "I don't like the way you made me, God." Instead we should remember Psalm 139:14 *(NLT)*: "Thank you for making me so wonderfully complex! Your workmanship is marvelous—and how well I know it."

And think about something else. Since he accepts us the way we are, we can say, "God, here's what really bothers me. What do you want me to know about it?"

That's a big question, isn't it? Take Christa, for instance. If she has good coordination, her height might help her become a basketball or volleyball star. But what if she doesn't have good coordination?

> I can choose to stop the target practice and look at God's promises instead!

It isn't what we don't have that's important. How we use what we do have is what really makes a difference. Maybe we begin to look at ourselves differently. Or maybe we learn to go on in spite of a real disability. Sometimes a disability forces us to accomplish a lot more than we would otherwise.

A great example of a person who was able to do this is Joni Eareckson Tada. When Joni was 17 years old, she dove into the Chesapeake Bay and broke her neck. She became a quadriplegic and was forced to live in a wheelchair. But she eventually discovered that, because of Christ, the things that looked like limits were transformed into huge gifts.

Joni learned to create awesome paintings by holding a brush in her mouth. She began speaking to thousands of people at Billy Graham missions. She became a gifted encourager who helps other people face difficult circumstances.

It isn't what we don't have that's important. How we use what we do have is what really makes a difference.

Joni has a great understanding of her life circumstances. She says, "Today as I look back, I am convinced that the whole ordeal of my paralysis was inspired by God's love. I wasn't the brunt of some cruel divine joke. God had *reasons* behind my suffering, and learning some of them has made all the difference in the world."

In 2 Corinthians 12 Paul says he's glad to have something physically wrong with him. Paul's weakness gave him the chance to learn how much God could help him. Paul's physical weakness also helped him have a stronger relationship with God.

In some cases the things we don't like about ourselves will be with us all our lives. With other problems we'll find that, as we grow older, what seemed like a big deal even can become something that helps us.

Often the girl who thinks she's too tall becomes the woman who is especially attractive because of the way she carries herself.

Or think about this. One day Tonya sat across a table from Julie, a woman whose eyes sparkled as she talked. Julie was lovely because she was so interested in listening to what Tonya had to say. But soon Tonya became aware of something else. She found herself listening not only to what Julie said, but also to how she said it.

When Tonya said, "You have a beautiful voice," Julie smiled and told her story.

"When I was growing up, my voice was so low that I dreaded having my music teacher test me in front of everyone else. Every time I sang a note, I sounded like a bullfrog. The other kids always laughed, and I was really embarrassed. When people like you tell me they like my voice, it means more to me than you can imagine!"

Maybe Julie understood what it meant to make herself a target. Do you suppose she also used word arrows that said, "There's something wrong with you?"

> But if we're just using ourselves for target practice, we can ask God to help us see ourselves the way he sees us.

When there is a real problem—a sin we need to deal with—we can confess it to God and ask forgiveness. But if we're just using ourselves for target practice, we can ask God to help us see ourselves the way he sees us.

And one more thing—we can ask him to use the things we don't like about ourselves for something good. Isn't that better than shooting arrows?

❀ Main Ingredient ❀

"My gracious favor is all you need. My power works best in your weakness." 2 Corinthians 12:9 *(NLT)*

❀ Temperature Control ❀

Lord, I ask your forgiveness for the things that aren't right in my life because they're really sin. Help me to turn from those sins and change. But with other kinds of things—when I compare myself to others or face a big disability—help me know the way you see me. And give me the courage to believe that you love me the way I am.

Dear Girlfriend,
Sometimes I feel really disappointed with people, don't you? I don't
like it—in fact, I hate being disappointed. But I'm starting to
wonder if it's just a part of life. A friend turns on me. someone
treats me unfairly, or a person I trusted breaks her word. When
that happens I wonder, "Does anybody care?" The answer is yes!
And that person, Jesus, knows exactly how you and I feel. The cool
thing is, he's only a whisper away. . . .

Good Night Superstar

❧ Recipe du Jour ❧

Quietly Carmen closed the back door. She paused for a
moment, looking around the kitchen. Voices were coming from
the family room.

Uh-oh! Gram's here, Carmen thought. *I don't feel like*
seeing anyone right now, not even her. Maybe I can sneak
upstairs to my room.

Halfway up, a stair creaked. "Is that you, Carmen?" her
mother called. "Gram would enjoy talking with you while I
start supper."

Inwardly Carmen groaned. *No way out of this one,* she
thought. Quickly she headed for her room, blew her nose,
wiped the tears from her eyes and cheeks, and pulled a brush
through her hair. When she went back downstairs to the family
room, she did her best to hide how upset she felt.

But two minutes later Grandma asked, "What's the matter, Carmen? Usually you're full of smiles."

Like a flood, it all spilled out. "Oh, Gram, you won't believe what happened. Heidi is having a slumber party Friday night, and she invited everyone but me!"

Carmen sniffed and Gram handed her a tissue. "All day long the girls were talking about how much fun it's going to be."

"Is Heidi someone you know well?" asked Gram.

That's the worst part. She used to be my best friend!

"That's the worst part," Carmen cried. "She used to be my best friend!"

"Oh, honey! That is awful, isn't it?"

"I used to like her." Carmen's throat felt tight again. "I used to tell her everything. Now I hate her. I feel like she punched me in the stomach!"

Like water breaking through a dam, Carmen could no longer hold back her tears. Gram waited, listening carefully. Finally Carmen spoke between sobs. "What should I do?"

Her grandma thought for a moment. "Well, I think it would help to be honest with God about how you feel."

"Oh, Gram, what good would that do?" Carmen wailed. "It's Heidi I'm mad at!"

"But God understands. That's one of the nice things about being able to pray. You can be honest with him."

> God understands. That's one of the nice things about being able to pray.

"Honest?" Carmen's laugh was hard and bitter. "If I were honest, I'd spit on Heidi. That's how I feel!"

When Gram laughed, Carmen scowled. "It's *not* funny!"

Her grandma grinned. "In my mind's eye, I just saw you gathering a mouthful of spit and meeting Heidi in the hallway at school."

Suddenly Carmen giggled. Then she had a thought. "Everyone in the whole school would know how upset I am, wouldn't they?"

Gram nodded.

"And if everyone knows how much it bothers me not to be invited . . . " Carmen thought about it. It wasn't hard to guess what would happen. "Things have a way of blowing up like a balloon ready to pop. Still, this one really hurt."

"Yes," Gram said quietly. "Sometimes life hurts." She gave Carmen a quick hug. "All of us want to believe in other people, but it's not always possible. People are human. Now and then they're going to hurt or disappoint us."

"That's for sure," Carmen agreed. "But what should I do about the party? Just sit here and take it?"

"Well . . . " Gram said slowly. "You've got another option. You could make a choice that would change your life."

Carmen knew what that was, and she didn't want to hear about it. Instead, she got up and stalked out of the family room. But later, when she was alone in her bedroom, tears

Burnt Cookies

again filled Carmen's eyes. As her tears brimmed over, thoughts of the party went around and around in her mind. Still upset, she turned out her light and pulled up the blinds before climbing into bed.

You could make a choice that would change your life.

A gentle breeze drifted in, bringing the fragrance of springtime through the half-open window. As Carmen lay there, she could see the night sky filled with stars. Moments later a cloud moved across the sky, hiding the stars. Then, just as quickly as the cloud came, it passed. Once again Carmen saw a clear sky with brilliant stars shining from a great distance. In that instant happiness welled up within her, pushing aside the aching hurt of the day.

The stars, she thought. *I'd forgotten, God. The stars are always there, even in the daytime when I can't see them. It's a reminder that you're always with me. Isn't it? For a while the clouds covered the stars, just like my hatred for Heidi. I was so mad at her that it blocked my view of you. But you never left me. Thanks for being a friend I can count on, no matter what happens.*

You never left me. You're a friend I can count on, no matter what happens.

In that moment Carmen remembered the discovery she'd made about God— how he loves each of us as individuals. How he sent his Son to die on the cross so that our sins won't stop that friendship from growing.

"Forgive me, Lord, for the way I hate Heidi for hurting me," Carmen prayed. "Take away my cloud of anger so I can see you again."

Then, as Carmen looked up into the night sky, she remembered the one bright star with which God had told the whole world of his Son's coming. As Carmen felt the tightness in her stomach start to go away, her lips parted in a smile.

"Thanks, Lord," she whispered. "When people disappoint me, I'm glad I can look to you. I guess a friend isn't real unless he's with me like you are—no matter how I feel."

For a brief moment the stars seemed to come closer. In her imagination Carmen felt as if she could reach out and touch them. Instead, she tucked one hand beneath her pillow. In a moment she was asleep, but her smile remained long after her tears had dried.

❀ Main Ingredient ❀

"God has said, 'I will never fail you. I will never forsake you.'" Hebrews 13:5 *(NLT)*

❀ Temperature Control ❀

When people disappoint me, help me to look at you, Lord, not at them. In your name, Jesus, I choose to forgive the person who hurt me. Thank you that because I've forgiven her, you will start changing my feelings. Big surprise! You'll even help me get over my hurt.

Here's what I think...

Dear Girlfriend,

You know what it's like. We want to do something new and exciting, but our parents say no. What is it with them, anyway? Are they telling us we aren't responsible enough? Do they think we can't handle the situation? They always say there's a reason behind the no, but . . . Do you suppose they're concerned about our safety or that something won't be good for us right now? I guess that God doesn't ask us to like every situation. Maybe he wants us to see it from their perspective. . . .

Friday Night Freedom

❀ Recipe du Jour ❀

Hannah leaned around the doorway. "Dad, you won't let me go to the movie, will you?"

Her dad looked up from the magazine he was reading. "What movie is it?" When Hannah told him, he answered, "No. I don't want you to see that."

"Good!" she said and returned to the phone.

"What was that all about?" Dad asked when Hannah finished talking with her friend. "I would have said no anyway, but you sent me a good signal."

Hannah grinned. "Oh, I really didn't want to go. I think the movie will be so scary that I'd have nightmares. But it sounds better if I tell my friends you said I couldn't go."

Burnt Cookies

Moms and dads can really help us, can't they? Sometimes what they want for us is really what we want for ourselves. Like Hannah, we find they can give us a good reason for saying no to things we're not sure we want to do. There are other times, though, when we really want to do something, but Mom or Dad tells us no. Then everything looks different! We feel like a fly buzzing at a screen, trying to get out. *What's the matter with Mom?* we wonder. *Why can't Dad see it my way? Why can't I have fun?*

> What's the matter with Mom? Why can't Dad see it my way? Why can't I have fun?

Sometimes we long to grow up, thinking that we will have the freedom to do whatever we like. Yet being mature is not always something that comes with birthdays. Maturity comes when we're able to handle responsibility. We may be responsible in some areas but not experienced enough in others.

> Maturity comes when we're able to handle responsibility. We may be responsible in some areas but not experienced enough in others.

We can find better ways to handle responsibility if we think about some of the reasons our parents say no. Leticia found a reason when she asked to go to a party at Danielle's house.

"Are Danielle's parents going to be home?" asked her dad.

"Well . . . I think so," said Leticia.

"Better find out for sure," he told her. "Otherwise the answer is no."

"But why?" Leticia asked. "We'll be all right. We're just ordering pizza and watching a couple of movies."

"And that's OK," agreed her dad. "But if there aren't any adults in the house, other kids might push you into something you can't handle."

Like Leticia, Cassie discovered that safety is important to her parents too. "I'd like to go to the game Friday night," she said.

> If our parents aren't willing to let us do something now, maybe they'll allow us to do something else.

Her mother turned from pulling clothes out of the dryer. "Where is it?"

Cassie named a nearby town. "I'm going with some older kids. Nicole's oldest sister will give us a ride."

"Is Nicole's sister used to driving after dark?"

Cassie sighed. *More questions!* "Sure, Mom. Quit worrying."

"How can I *not* worry?" Her mom put down the towel she was folding. "I'll probably never forget something that happened when I was your age. Four girls from my school drove to a game. Coming home they were in a bad car accident and two of them were killed."

"Oh, Mom, how morbid! Why do you have to think of things like that?"

Cassie's mom handed her some towels to fold. "Look," she

said. "I want you to have fun at the game. But we need to work out some rules. I'd feel better knowing you took the bus instead of riding with someone I don't know is a good driver."

Sometimes our parents say no because they think we're too young. That's a bitter pill to swallow. And perhaps the only cure is to wait until we're a bit older to take on certain rights and responsibilities. But there's a bright side. If our parents aren't willing to let us do something now, maybe they will allow us to do something else.

Leticia has learned it helps to ask in a nice tone of voice. Sometimes it's possible to work out a compromise. "It still makes me mad when my parents won't let me do things," she said. "It took me a long time to understand why, but now I enjoy some things more because Mom and Dad made me wait to try them."

When we know why our mom or dad says no, it helps us understand why God wants us to obey them.

Sometimes following rules is a matter of life or death. Most parents want rules about riding with a new driver. How long has someone had her license? How much driving experience has she had? How many kids will be in the car?

When we know why our mom or dad says no, it helps us understand why God wants us to obey our parents. Of course there are times when that seems next to impossible, because their saying no doesn't change how much we want to do something. Yet God promises happiness to those who obey their parents. And when we do obey, we learn something more—how much they love us.

❀ Main Ingredient ❀

"Honor your father and mother, as the LORD your God commanded you. Then you will live a long, full life in the land the LORD your God will give you." Deuteronomy 5:16 *(NLT)*

❀ Temperature Control ❀

Lord, when I'm upset because my parents say no, help me understand how they feel. Help us to figure out rules that will work for both them and me.

Here's what I think...

Dear Girlfriend,
Sometimes it's tough, isn't it? The ads, TV, our friends—everyone tells us what to wear, how to act, how to feel. The pressure gets so intense it seems like it would be easier just to give in to whatever we're tempted to do. Plus, it's hard to stand alone. But the cool thing is—we don't have to. We've got someone who'll stand up with us and stick by us—no matter what. . . .

Contents Under Pressure

❀ Recipe du Jour ❀

"What is it with you? Don't you know? Everybody's doing it!"

Ever been the target of those words? If you don't give in, you feel like a green bug others are just waiting to stomp on.

Sooner or later all of us are going to be tempted to do something that is wrong or harmful to ourselves. "Everybody's doing it" is a phrase that often pops into our minds when we're being tempted. What counts is how we respond to that temptation.

A small part of us might think, *That sounds like a good time. I'd really like to try that.* The moment those thoughts start, we have to work hard not to let them win. Saying no is seldom easy, especially if friends are doing the asking! The more we like people, the harder it is to turn them down. It's

> *What counts is how we respond to temptation.*

scary to think we might have to stand alone.

When a teacher asked his class a question, DJ gave the opposite answer from everyone else. The rest of the class laughed at him.

"You're wrong!" they said. But DJ defended his answer and gave reasons for his choice. One by one the others fell silent as they realized he was right, even though he stood alone. Because DJ thought about his answers and knew where to stand, he was able to achieve huge goals.

Standing up for what you believe is like paddling a canoe. We begin on one side of a lake. Our destination is a point on the other side. To reach it we pick out a tall pine tree and keep the bow of the canoe pointed in that direction. The waves become choppy, and it seems rough going. But as we keep our eyes on the tree and paddle hard, we finally arrive where we want to be.

When standing alone doesn't feel worth it, we can ask ourselves, "What do I want to be doing five years from now?" And then, "Am I being tempted by something that will keep me from reaching that goal?"

Whatever temptation is involved—whether it's smoking, getting involved with sex, or experimenting with alcohol or other drugs—keeping these questions in mind can help us avoid doing things that will damage our future.

Battling temptation often involves the small, two-letter word *no*. Learning to say no is an important part of growing up. Some adults still have trouble turning down things that people try to push them into. When we say no to something that can hurt us, we build our self-respect. One step at a time, our good choices help us become responsible adults. As Lindsey put it, "Others will have to respect my right to say no."

Sometimes there's more involved than just saying no once. Today everyone knows that smoking leads to cancer. When Monica's friends asked the first time, "Want to go for a smoke?" she answered, "I'll walk with you, but I'll pass on the cigarettes."

Monica's friends didn't make a big deal about it, but they kept asking her to smoke. After a month of being asked, Monica started smoking.

We might have some friends we need to stay away from. If we let them keep hounding us, it's like trying to straddle a fence. On one side there's green grass. On the other, a pile of rocks. If we don't remove ourselves from tempting situations, eventually we'll have to jump one way or another. If we land on the rocky pile, we'll get scrapes and bruises.

I like knowing that God has a plan for me.

Yolanda discovered that the sooner she says no, the better. She finds it easier to make a good choice right away. She also wants to make that choice before trying something that could become a harmful habit. "I want to be honest with myself," she said. "I need to admit that I'm not able to handle things alone. But when I ask for God's help, I can't keep swinging one way or another. I need to make the hard choices and stick to them. I like knowing that God has a plan for me."

When we're tempted, the Holy Spirit will give us the power we need to say no. All we have to do is ask God for help. That's what Caitlin did when she didn't want to go along with what her friends were doing. When they called her a wimp, she offered a quick silent prayer with her eyes open. *Lord, this is too big for me. Help!* But then she had to do what he showed her. She walked out of temptation's reach.

❀ Main Ingredient ❀

"Be strong with the Lord's mighty power." Ephesians 6:10 *(NLT)*

❀ Temperature Control ❀

Thanks, Lord, that when I'm tempted, you will give me the power to say no. Help me also to walk out of temptation's reach.

Dear Girlfriend,
I don't like to lose or feel rejected. You're the same way, aren't you? It seems like all of us want to win and be successful at what we do. But how can we cruise through life and avoid all the potholes? Can you help me keep something in mind? When I feel that I've wound up at the side of the road—or even worse—in the ditch, I want to remember that God is holding my life map. There may be a detour ahead. . . .

Burnt Cookies

❀ Recipe du Jour ❀

"You should have seen how scared I was the first time I tried to ride a horse," said Jessica. "And sure enough, I fell off."

All of us know the sinking feeling that comes when we try our best but fail anyway. Like when we're on a girls' softball team and strike out, losing the game, instead of hitting the winning run. Or when we come in just a few points too low for the grade we need to pass a test. When we fail at something we really wanted to do, we can't help but feel discouraged. Maybe our best isn't good enough—or is it? How can we deal with our failures?

> Could it be that what seems like failure will someday turn into success?

We have two choices. We can hang our heads and say, "That's it! I'm never going to try that again." Or we can take our mistakes and learn something from them. We all know that failing is no fun, but could it be that what seems like failure will someday turn into success?

The smell of burning cookies filled the kitchen. Megan snatched up a pot holder, yanked open the oven door, and grabbed the pan. But it was too late. The charred mess was hopeless. Feeling disgusted with herself, Megan took the pan to the sink and sent her burnt offering down the disposal.

What a mess! she thought. *What's Mom going to say? I better make sure it doesn't happen again.*

Like Megan, we can let our failures remind us to concentrate more on what we're doing. But there are other times when we concentrate very hard, give our best effort, and still fail.

> There are times when learning to lose is more important than winning.

We'd always like to win or succeed, but there are times when learning to lose is more important than winning. Sometimes losing forces us to change our goals.

Brianna had worked hard to learn the school cheers. She thought that her handsprings and somersaults were perfect. But when she didn't make the cheerleading squad, she decided not to sit around.

"I signed up to paint props for the school play," she said. "At first I just filled in where others had drawn a shape, but soon I learned how to sketch things out." Later on, Brianna decided she wanted to learn more about painting. Now she's thinking about becoming a professional artist.

Failing might also push us to work harder and accomplish something important. One girl who nearly drowned three different times pushed herself to become an excellent swimmer. Another girl, Emily, envied one of her friends because she could make everyone laugh. "I really wanted to do that too," Emily said. "But whenever I told a joke, I forgot the punch line, and it fell flat." She decided there were other things she could do well.

> Failing might also push us to work harder and accomplish something important.

Katie was embarrassed that she'd flunked an English test. That same day a teacher told her to leave class because she was whispering and giggling too much. She sat in the principal's office and thought about where she was headed. "I'm really not succeeding at being the class clown. And I know I could get good grades if I tried."

After that Katie started working hard at school. Soon her grades showed everyone that she was more than the class clown. At the end of the year, she even received an award for doing so well in school.

"I used to feel really bad every time I failed," Katie said. "Now, even though it's hard, I keep trying to learn something when I fail. I want to depend on God's help."

Depending on God and believing in his best can sometimes be hard to do, can't it? When Jesus walked and talked

Burnt Cookies

with his disciples, they thought he would become king of their world. When he died on the cross, they felt they had lost everything, including their best friend. But Jesus surprised them by rising from the dead.

I want to depend on God's help.

Burnt cookies? A lost game? Could what seems like a loss turn into a gain? And what happened to Jessica after falling off the horse? She got back on. In time she had her own horse and started riding in competitions. She even became the champion of a six-state region!

❀ Main Ingredient ❀

"And we know that God causes everything to work together for the good of those who love God and are called according to his purpose for them." Romans 8:28 *(NLT)*

❀ Temperature Control ❀

Thanks, Jesus, that even when I fail, you can bring something good out of it. In those times when I seem to lose, show me how to depend on you and believe in your best. Help me remember that your Good Friday became Easter morning.

Breathing Room

❀ Recipe du Jour ❀

Erin yawned, fumbled for the light switch, and struggled to
open her eyes. The last thing she felt like doing was getting
out of bed. *Why do some days have to be so hard?* she asked
herself. *A paper due in English. A test in math. A report for sci-
ence. Yuck! It's not worth getting up.*

All of us have had those days, right? Times when we wonder if we're going to get anything done, let alone everything.
Times when our muscles tighten just thinking about the work
that is expected of us.

Now and then things seem hard because we're short on
sleep. And sometimes people push us because they know
we're able to do more than we're doing. But for Erin there was
another problem. She solved it by learning to ask herself a
question: *Am I doing my best at the right time, or am I waiting*

until the pressure is on to try to pull something off?

Putting things off until the last minute causes stress we don't need to face. If we're already in that moment, it's too late for much help. Before letting ourselves get pushed beyond what we can handle, we might ask, *Am I taking on too much?*

All of us have a certain amount of things we have to do. We need to help out at home, for instance. In school we often don't have a choice about how much work we must do. We're required to do a certain amount. And sometimes we need to do extra credit projects to raise our grade.

Am I doing my best at the right time, or am I waiting until the pressure is on to try to pull something off?

Usually it's in other kinds of things that we need to make choices. Adults face the same problem. You may have heard your mom or dad say, "Oh, I wish I hadn't agreed to do that!"

Annie is gifted in many ways and finds it hard to decide how much she can handle. She likes band and choir, plays on the volleyball team, baby-sits, and helps plan events for her church youth group. She likes taking part in different kinds of groups. Being in a number of activities is fun!

But even something that starts out being fun can drag us down if it's another leaf dropped on a pile that's already too high. While it's not good to say no all the time, it's also not good to say yes all the time. So what can we do?

Let's ask another question: *Do I have any quiet moments in my life?* In other words, *Do I take the time just to be still and think for a bit?* Davika has a tree with spreading branches where she likes to sit and read. That's where she thinks, too, and she has big thoughts and a good imagination. When it's good weather, she takes her Bible there, and Jesus has become her best friend.

Do I have any quiet moments in my life? Do I take the time just to be still and think for a bit?

It helps to find balance in our lives when we decide, *What is really important to me?* Notice what you enjoy doing. It might be a sport you especially like or taking part in a musical activity. But you might also like to give some time to a person who needs help. There's a lot of satisfaction in that.

Other times we need to ask, *Am I a self-starter?* A self-starter gets started even when no one tells her she must. It's easy to wait on beginning homework until mom or dad reminds us. Mei Ling is just the opposite. Most likely she will do well in whatever she chooses to do. In many jobs and activities it's important to be a self-starter and just begin doing what needs to be done.

"If I keep putting something off it feels like a bigger job than it really is," Mei Ling says. "It's easier to get things done on my own than to have my parents nag me." She grinned. "Don't get me wrong. I don't like homework. But if I didn't have to go to school I'd be bored with vacation."

Part of being a self-starter means being able to set priorities—to decide the best order to do things. Try another question: *Do I always tackle the hardest job first?* Often it helps to

Burnt Cookies

get the job we dislike most out of the way, because once we're tired it'll seem impossible to do.

"If I can deal with the hardest job, then I know I can do the easiest!" Cara says. "It's fun to reward myself at the end— maybe by having a friend over or doing something else that I like."

Often it helps to get the job we dislike most out of the way, because once we're tired it'll seem impossible to do.

It's also necessary to ask ahead of time, *When is my deadline?* Cara uses a little time-planning trick. "I set a time before something is really due. If I can't quite make my deadline, I still have a little time left before the real deadline."

Then there's something else that's important to ask ourselves: *Am I trying to be perfect or trying to do my best?"*

If we're trying to reach perfection, we don't give ourselves a chance to make a mistake now and then. If instead we try to do our best, we give ourselves a little breathing room. We can get up and start over again.

"Just because something is easy for others, doesn't mean I can do it perfectly," Erin says. "But," she adds, "I can always do my best."

If we're trying to reach perfection, we don't give ourselves a chance to make a mistake now and then.

Perhaps in time we'll discover another secret. If we give ourselves some breathing room, we may no longer feel as pushed. And if we make quiet times a part of each day, we'll feel better about the rest of the day. Erin discovered a surprise: "Sometimes I even have extra minutes I didn't count on."

❀ Main Ingredient ❀

"God has given each of us the ability to do certain things well." Romans 12:6 *(NLT)*

❀ Temperature Control ❀

Guide me, Lord, in how I spend my time so I make the best use of the abilities you have given me. Help me become a self-starter.

Here's what I think...

Dear Girlfriend,
Sometimes it feels like I'll never have enough—enough clothes,
DVDs, sports equipment—you know, stuff. Why is it that some of our
friends seem to have everything? Do they get a bigger allowance?
Do their parents make more money? It's easy to want something so
badly that we're willing to do anything to get it. God promises to
cover all our needs, but what about our "wants"? Can some of our
"needs" really be "wants" in disguise? . . .

My Good Life

❀ Recipe du Jour ❀

Tarah felt the hotness creep up into her cheeks. Words seemed to fill the room, beating against her head. The first time she shoplifted, she had been with other kids. They had wanted to see if they could get away with it.

Now the store manager asked, "Have you stolen anything before?" He and Tarah sat in his office. The jacket she had taken lay on a table nearby.

Unable to speak, Tarah nodded. The first time she shoplifted had been on a dare from her friends. It seemed exciting to get new clothes without paying for them. Today her friends were with her again, and she had taken a really expensive jacket. But there was something Tarah worried about more than getting caught. *If I give my friends away, I'll be in really big trouble!*

Burnt Cookies

Tarah fixed her gaze on her favorite ring. As she twisted it around and around her finger, she hoped the manager would get this over with fast.

Instead he asked, "What did you take when you shoplifted before?"

Tarah swallowed hard. "Some little things," she said in a small voice. "It seemed like no big deal."

It seemed like no big deal.

"That's what most kids tell me," the manager said. "But it is a big deal to someone. Can you guess who?"

Instead of meeting his eyes, Tarah looked through the open doorway into the store. Every shelf seemed full to overflowing. The people who owned the store must be rich to have all that. They wouldn't miss what she took. "But you have so much."

"And the store has to pay for everything. When kids shoplift it cuts into our profit—the money that helps us stay open. If a store can't stay open, we lose our jobs. It hurts our families."

Tarah took another quick glance through the door. He had a family? Maybe even kids her age? She had never thought about shoplifting in that way. That it could actually hurt who-ever owned or managed the store.

"But there's more," the shopkeeper said. "When you take something that doesn't belong to you, it's stealing. You're set-ting a pattern for the kind of person you will become. Is this who you want to be?"

When Tarah answered, her voice was small. "Today I came in because I wanted something and didn't have enough money to pay for it."

"Very few of us can have everything we want," the manager answered. "When we catch a shoplifter, I usually call the police. Because I know your parents, I'll ask them to come get you. But instead of putting what you stole back on the shelf, I'm going to ask you to pay for it. I expect you to come in each week with a certain amount of money until you've paid for the jacket you stole. Then you can take it home."

When Tarah groaned, the manager asked, "Does it still seem like no big deal?"

Tarah finally met his eyes. "No," she said. But she knew something more. *All that work to pay for something, and I won't like wearing the jacket. I'll remember this instead!*

"If I catch you wanting something again without paying for it, I'll make a different telephone call."

Tarah's fingers trembled. "I'll get arrested?" she asked, twisting her ring again.

The manager nodded. "If you keep stealing things, your arrests will give you a police record that will follow you the rest of your life."

Perhaps Tarah is like some of us. We don't always realize when something that seems small is actually very big. Not being able to control our wants can hurt us many years later.

We can have good goals that help us move forward and reach the place where we want to be. It's like using in-line skates. They help us get where we want to go much faster than if we walked. Or we can have wants that push us back-ward.

We don't always realize when something that seems small is actually very big.

"If I want too much or want the wrong things, my wants can hurt me," Brie said. "I'm in too big a hurry."

It's like hitting a patch of sand and wiping out. If we slide out of control, we end up with skinned knees and elbows.

What's more, there will always be someone who has more than we do. Adults face this problem all the time. They see neighbors and friends with bigger houses, newer cars, and nicer clothes. And sometimes grown-ups fall into the trap of wanting what their neighbors have. But guess what?

It's a matter of deciding whether we'll allow our wants to control us. Or whether we'll control our wants.

If we want to escape the same trap, we can begin right now, while we're young. It's a matter of deciding whether we'll allow our wants to control us. Or whether we'll control our wants.

Sometimes our wants take the form of new games, special clothes, a tennis racket, snowboard, or skis. None of these is bad in itself. It's the attitude we have that counts. Let's ask ourselves, "Why are these things important to me? What is my goal in getting them?"

Brittany explained, "It's like picking petals from a flower and doing the 'he loves me—he loves me not' thing. Instead, I make a list of what I want and say, 'I want this—I can't afford that. It helps me figure out the things I really want to save money for."

Many kids already know how to make their money stretch. Karin is one of them. "I save my allowance and earn extra money by baby-sitting," she says. Then Karin waits until she's sure how she wants to spend it. She's learned to sew, and she makes jewelry for herself and others. Because she hangs onto her money she had a big surprise. When the family of one of her friends invited her to go on a special trip, Karin already had half of the money she needed. That made it easier for her parents to add the other half and say yes!

❀ Main Ingredient ❀

"Choose today whom you will serve. . . . But as for me and my family, we will serve the Lord.'" Joshua 24:15 *(NLT)*

❀ Temperature Control ❀

Forgive me, Lord, for the times I've wanted more than is good for me. Help me to know the difference between a want and a need. Help me to be in control of my money and my wants.

Here's what I think...

Dear Girlfriend,
I've been thinking about the people who bug me most. What about
you? Is it your younger brother or sister or the bully down the street?
Or maybe one of the most popular girls at school? It's tough trying
to get along with others. Sometimes it's hard to figure out where
they're coming from. It's even harder to be willing to be the bigger
person. It takes practice, doesn't it? . . .

War Zone

❀ Recipe du Jour ❀

Ashley felt the frustration churning within her. "My little brother bugs me! My sister wants to do everything I do! And the
kids at school are picking on me!" Familiar problems? For most
of us, they are all too familiar. There can be several reasons
why it's hard to get along with others.

We might start by wondering, *Why does my little brother
or sister get into my stuff?* It may be that they're too little to
know better. But that's hard to believe when they put a frog in
your bed or rip the guts out of your favorite stuffed animal!

"One day I saw my little sister combing her hair the way I
comb mine," said Casey. "Then a little while later I flopped
down on my beanbag. My little sister doesn't have a beanbag,
but she sat down on the floor too—trying to lean back just the
way I did."

Burnt Cookies

Maybe the bugging and following around give us a clue about how much they really admire us. Of course, no younger brother or sister would admit that. Not for anything! Yet Ashley discovered that if she spent some time trying to make the younger members of her family feel loved, all of them usually got along better.

"Often I give them some of my things—things I'm too old for anyway," she said. "They really like that."

In addition to sharing, it often helps to set boundaries. If we have a room of our own, we might talk to Mom or Dad about how to do that. If we share a room, it helps to have a shelf where we can put the things that are important to us. Mom or Dad will probably be willing to tell a little sister that she can't touch anything on that shelf.

But now and then trouble comes not because of our things being wrecked, but because others want their own way. Angelina often baby-sits and knows that the 3-year-old she cares for will get cranky if she doesn't put him to bed on time.

"When I first was with him, he always said, 'I won't do it!' to anything I'd suggest. Now I've learned a few tricks to avoid power struggles. I start getting him ready for bed early enough so that his worst side doesn't have time to come out. Instead of saying, 'Go to bed now,' I tell him, 'When you're in bed, I'll read a story.' And I make it interesting, so he looks forward to reading whenever I come."

In addition to sharing, it often helps to set boundaries.

If sparks are flying with a younger brother or sister, it sometimes helps to consider the source. "I get so mad that it's hard to chill out about things," Megan said. "Yet I know I'm the only one who can do it. Often what my little brother really wants is an out—he knows he's wrong, but he still has to fight to the end. The best way to stop it is if I can figure out a way to help him save face."

A different problem comes when we're involved with someone our own age or older—someone who puts us down every chance she gets. Usually the problem isn't really ours. It belongs to the one doing the teasing. Often she doesn't feel good about herself, and looks for ways to make others feel bad. Then it becomes our problem because some teasing hurts. At times the best cure is to ignore mean words until the person saying them gives up trying to bug us.

At times the best cure is to ignore mean words until the person saying them gives up trying to bug us.

Other times a good solution is to find a compromise. We make a mistake when we feel we must compete with everyone and always win. Every week on the same night two sisters fought over the TV. Each had a favorite show during a certain time slot. At last, tired of the hassle, one of them said, "OK, I'll let you watch your show this week. But then you let me watch mine next week."

It takes a big person to put away what she wants and back down. Now and then both people can win by working out a way to do things together. At other times the only way to stop fighting is to admit that we aren't perfect. No one is right 100 percent of the time.

> Now and then both people can win by working out a way to do things together.

"I guess the best way to get along with others is to get along with myself," said Megan. "Part of that is being willing to say, 'I'm sorry. Will you forgive me?'"

Getting along with others can be like walking a tightrope. The high wire artist in a circus can't lean too far to the left or to the right without falling off. In the same way, God doesn't expect us to bend over so far that we become something we really aren't. He wants us to find a place in the middle where we can agree.

> When Jesus could have backed away from the reason he came to Earth, he chose to walk to the cross.

God also doesn't expect us to turn into a doormat and let people walk all over us. Neither does he want us to give in and do something we know is wrong. Guess who understood how to do all that balancing? Jesus!

Remember how he overturned tables and threw the moneychangers out of the temple? He knew the temple was his Father's holy house. But in a different situation, Jesus remained silent. When Jesus could have backed away from the reason he came to Earth, he chose to walk to the cross. He chose to die there for us so that we can receive forgiveness for our sins, salvation, and eternal life. Pretty awesome, isn't it?

❀ Main Ingredient ❀

"God saved you by his special favor when you believed. And you can't take credit for this; it is a gift from God." Ephesians 2:8 *(NLT)*

❀ Temperature Control ❀

Thank you, Lord, for loving me, even during the times when I'm not easy to love. Thank you for loving me so much that you died on the cross to save me from my sins. I want you to be my Savior and to be Lord over every part of my life. I want to enjoy your forgiveness, your salvation, and eternal life with you. I can't wait!

Here's what I think...

Dear Girlfriend,
I like having a friend like you, even though you can't be with me all
the time! Picking and choosing the right friends is really important.
Both of us know that, while it's great to be in a group where every-
body likes doing the same things, not all groups are good for us.
And sometimes learning to be a good friend is an even bigger
challenge. . . .

Sole Survivor

❀ Recipe du jour ❀

Trays thudded onto tables and silverware clattered. Voices
filled the lunchroom, rising and falling in waves of sound.
Kelsey stood at the end of the cafeteria line, balancing her tray
and looking in all directions.

Loneliness grabbed at her stomach as she wondered
where to go. All around her, small groups huddled. But
where could she sit? None of her friends ate at
the same time she did.

Most of us have faced a situation like
Kelsey's. We know the empty
feeling of being left out. It's natural to
want to be part of a group where we
belong. God created us in such a way that
we need other people. Yet we discover that groups
have a way of molding us.

> It's a natural feeling to want to be part of a group where we belong.

Burnt Cookies

So how can we become part of a group that would be helpful to us? "By looking for friends in the right places," Jennifer said.

As we meet people in different groups, we learn to size them up. We can ask ourselves, "What is this group all about? Does it have the values that are important to Jesus and to me?" If so, we can decide, *That's a group I want to be a part of.* If not, we're free to think, *It doesn't really matter if I gain their approval or not.*

> When we feel uncomfortable with a group, it's often for a good reason.

When we we're uncomfortable with a group, it's often for a good reason. It's better to leave a group than to stay just because we want to fit in *somewhere*.

Groups can offer surprises. On the surface they may seem shiny and valuable like gemstones. They may look attractive and appear to be the best. Yet these groups may not be made up of the people that are the right friends for us.

Other groups are like geodes—ordinary, plain-looking rocks. Shaped like a ball with a rough gray-white surface, there's nothing showy on the outside. Yet when a rock cutter splits a geode in half, there's a big surprise. In the blue and purple hollow inside, a geode is full of beautiful crystals. Those crystals are like the valuable friendships that are possible with the right friends.

If we're part of a group offering the right kind of friendship, we can just be ourselves. You might be thinking,

Yeah, right! Easier said than done. But there are certain telltale signs that can give away the fact that we're trying too hard.

> If we're part of a group offering the right kind of friendship, we can just be ourselves.

"I always giggled too much," one girl said. "I was trying to attract attention by being sure everyone knew I was having fun."

"I guess I bragged all the time," remarked another girl. "I thought they'd want me along if I made myself look good."

When asked what happened, she grinned. "They didn't want me at all. They thought I was trying to be better than them."

A third girl spoke up. "I used to act really pushy—pushing myself into places where I hadn't earned the right to be. I don't do that anymore. Sometimes friendships take time. I want others to like me because I'm me. When they do, they'll let me in."

At times the hardest part of being ourselves is to keep from freezing up when we feel left out. "I always put on a bored look—just for self-defense," said Kelsey. "Sometimes I didn't look at kids when they talked. That's what they told me anyway. Then everyone thought I wasn't interested in being friends."

"That's kind of what I did too," Destiny said. "I always waited for someone to come to me. I didn't realize I was just looking at myself. Then I learned to reach out to other kids."

Destiny likes being part of her home-schooling group. When they meet together for sports or a special class session, she looks for a person who might not know the other girls and tries to help her feel welcome.

And what about being new in a school or community? Often it's easier to make friends with girls who are also new. While others in a class have known each other a long time, people who are new to an area need each other. To get acquainted it helps to ask questions about what the other person likes to do.

As we reach out and show an interest in others, our shyness will go away. If there's an opportunity to help someone, let's jump to it! Often we become part of a group by being friends with one of its members.

> As we reach out and show an interest in others, our shyness will go away.

Soon after Samantha moved into a new neighborhood, she saw a girl walking her dog around the block. When school started a few mornings later, she learned that the girl's name was Beth and that they rode the same bus to school. Yet each time Beth spoke to her, Samantha froze. She wanted so much to be part of Beth's group that she couldn't think of anything to say. Beth misunderstood and thought that Samantha didn't want to be friends. Whenever they got on the bus, she went to the back and joined a group of girls while Samantha sat alone near the front.

Then one day Samantha was sitting on her front steps when Beth was out walking her dog. Just as they passed the house, the dog saw a squirrel. Suddenly the dog bounded forward, pulling the leash out of Beth's hands. When she ran after him, trying to catch his collar, the dog edged away. Samantha jumped off the steps and moved quietly over behind the dog. Just before she reached him, he saw her and streaked around the house.

"Sorry," she said to Beth. "Why don't you go one way? I'll go another. Maybe we can corner him."

Each took off in a different direction. Finally, Beth grabbed the dog's collar.

"Hey, thanks for helping," she said. "He's terrible when he gets loose." She smiled shyly. "You know, I used to think that you were stuck on yourself."

"But not anymore?" asked Samantha.

Beth smiled again. "Not anymore."

❀ Main Ingredient ❀

"There are 'friends' who destroy each other, but a real friend sticks closer than a brother." Proverbs 18:24 *(NLT)*

❀ Temperature Control ❀

Thanks, Lord, for understanding my need for friends. Guide me so that I become part of the right groups. Help me to be a true friend to others.

Here's what I think...

Dear Girlfriend,
Sometimes change is fun, but sometimes it's really awful, isn't it?
Especially when change comes because of a divorce. It's easy to
think that our parents don't love us anymore. And a girl can't help
but wonder: Where will I live? What will happen to our family? Who
will take care of me? For anyone going through divorce, things are
tough, but there's still good news too. . . .

Splitsville

❀ Recipe du Jour ❀

Since early that morning nothing had gone right for Jackie. And
now this! She sat in a kitchen chair, a cold shiver running
through her even though the day was warm. She looked from
her mom to her dad.

"You're really getting a divorce?" she asked. "But what
about me? Mom, if I live with you, when will I see Dad?"

Then she felt the tears pressing against her eyes. Jackie
jumped up, headed for her room, and slammed the door
before her parents could see her cry. As she buried her head
in her pillow, sobs shook her body.

Why? Why? Why? she asked herself. *I should have
guessed. They've acted strangely for so long. They never seem
to talk to each other.*

Then the reality hit her. I did know. I just wouldn't face it.
Once again Jackie began sobbing. As she tried to catch

her breath, another thought struck her. *Do they love me anymore?*

She had cried for what seemed forever when she heard her mom calling through the door. "Jackie! Let's talk, OK?"

Slowly Jackie stood up and opened the door. When she fell into her mother's arms, it seemed that Mom needed the hug as much as she did.

Many of us have parents who are happy being together. But others of us may be in Jackie's situation. If we're living with two people whose marriage is falling apart, it's natural to wonder how their decision to separate will affect us. It helps to remember that marriage and divorce are between two adults. Something has changed the way they feel about each other. But that feeling is one kind of love. The love they have for us as their children is something entirely different.

If we're living with two people whose marriage is falling apart, it's natural to wonder how their decision to separate will affect us.

"I learned that both my parents still love me very much," said one girl whose parents were divorced. "That was something that stayed the same even when Mom moved out of our house."

We may never know the real reason behind our parents' desire to live separate lives.

We may never know the real reason behind our parents' desire to live separate lives. Yet, whatever it is, we can say to ourselves, "They love me now, and they'll keep on loving me, no matter what happens."

If our parents are planning a divorce, there are some things that might help us face what is happening. We'll feel better if we realize how much our parents need us.

Mom and dad are also being hurt by what is happening. Some time ago they joined their lives together in marriage—a gift that God has given to a man and a woman. But something has gone wrong. A tight band around their hearts is squeezing the love they once had for each other. The fun they used to share is missing. Their lives are empty, and they need to hear us say, "I love you, Mom. I love you, Dad."

> This is one of those times when we need to talk to someone about what's happening.

We might also discover that this is one of those times when we need to talk to someone about what's happening. Perhaps we feel we can talk to one of our parents. If not, sometimes a close friend can help. Usually, though, it's better to find an adult who will understand how we feel. We might choose the mother of one of our friends, a favorite teacher at church or school, or our youth minister. We should feel free to say, "My mom and dad are getting a divorce, and I'm upset."

And then there's something else we can do. It's normal to feel badly when we learn that something as important as our family is going to be different. We feel as though we've climbed a tree and the branch underneath us is splitting. But that's where our best friend, Jesus, comes in again. He loves us and will help us no matter what is happening. We can pray, "Lord, help me face whatever changes my life might bring."

Burnt Cookies

Things might be really tough right now, but the good news is that our heavenly Father loves us. He knows all about the situation and wants to help.

One girl felt led by God to take a bold step. Soon after her parents told her they were getting a divorce, she said to her father, "Dad, I'm sorry you and mom feel that way. Do you mind if I pray about it?" As she prayed about the situation, God's love began to fill their home again.

> We should feel free to say, "My mom and dad are getting a divorce, and I'm upset about it."

Perhaps we, too, can hope for that to still happen. But when we pray, we need to remember that this is a grown-up choice, not ours, to make. And what is most important of all? That if we invite him, God will be with us in every situation.

❀ Main Ingredient ❀

"Don't worry about anything; instead, pray about everything. Tell God what you need, and thank him for all he has done." Philippians 4:6 *(NLT)*

❀ Temperature Control ❀

Lord, thank you that I can tell you about our needs as a family. Help us to love one another. Use the hard times in our lives to help us grow deeper in you.

Dear Girlfriend,
It's easy to get upset when our parents ask questions about where we're going and who our friends are. Sometimes it feels like they don't trust us, right? I guess they just want to know that we're being responsible. How are you handling that? It sure can take a lot of practice. . . .

Olympic Gold!

❀ Recipe du Jour ❀

"I feel bugged all the time," complained Annie.

"What's the matter?" asked her friend Jill.

"I want to be me and do the things I feel like doing."

"Oh, sure. Me too," answered Jill. "I know what you mean. I get tired of all the questions from my parents. 'What time are you coming in? Where are you going? Who are you going with?' One night we talked it all out."

"You and your mom and dad?"

Jill nodded. "They said they were questioning me because they really didn't feel they could trust me."

"Trust you?"

"Sure. They figured I didn't know how to take care of myself. They wondered if I could make good choices," said Jill.

Isn't it easy to feel like we're being given the third degree when our parents question us? And it's hard to remember that many grown-ups feel as Jill's parents did. They're asking themselves, "Can I trust her to make the right choices when I'm not around to help?"

Trust is a funny thing. Like the ability of an Olympic figure skater, trust takes a long time to develop. Yet if we do the wrong thing, trust can quickly be lost. Most of us want to be an Olympic medal winner when it comes to making choices. But how can we get our parents to trust us?

Jill realizes that her mom and dad like to know where she's going and when she'll be back. If they're home, she tells them before they have a chance to ask. When they aren't around, she leaves a note on the kitchen table. "Went to Holly's," she writes. "Be back in time for supper."

When we love someone, we want to know that person is safe. And parents have been in the habit of loving us for a long time. Parents also appreciate it if we are able to keep a promise. "It seems as if I'm always late," moaned Mary. "I really mean to get in on time, but I never make it."

Having a sense of timing helps us no matter how old we are. Sometimes it's hard to judge how long it's going to take us

> Like the ability of an Olympic figure skater, trust takes a long time to develop.

> When we love someone, we want to know that person is safe. And parents have been in the habit of loving us for a long time.

Having a sense of
timing helps us no
matter how old we are.

to get to a certain place. Yet if we give ourselves a few extra minutes as a cushion, we'll usually come out all right.

Our parents also need to know if our plans change. At the last moment, Whitney discovered that the party had been moved to Andrea's house. Andrea's dad gave her a ride there, but during the evening, Whitney forgot to call her dad and give him the new address where she should be picked up.

After 45 minutes of waiting and circling the block where he thought the party was, her father went home. Feeling concerned and angry, he began calling other parents, asking, "Do you know where Whitney and the others are?"

Another girl, Sara, knows something else about building trust with her parents.

"Hey, let's go to my house," she said after school. "My mom won't mind if we make some snacks—that is, if we don't make too big a mess." Sara realizes her mother likes it when she invites friends over. Most moms do. It gives them a chance to see that we know how to pick our friends. And that's another thing that makes them feel better about the choices we make.

What does being worthy
of trust really amount to?

So, what does being worthy of trust really amount to? Simply living up to the best that is within us. It's feeling a sense of responsibility toward everyone who loves us. It's also realizing that we can't make exceptions for ourselves, thinking we can get away with something we shouldn't.

And that brings us back to the problem of feeling bugged by questions. We might still ask, "Will my parents stop bothering me if I do all these things?" Well, no one can guarantee what will happen with every mom or dad. But what do we have to lose? Maybe if they know how thoughtful we are about the things they can see, they'll trust us with more of the things they *can't* see! And won't that prove our ability to reach for the Olympic gold?

❋ Main Ingredient ❋

"Those who obey God's word really do love him. That is the way to know whether or not we live in him. Those who say they live in God should live their lives as Christ did."
1 John 2:5, 6 *(NLT)*

❋ Temperature Control ❋

Remind me, Lord, of my responsibility to those who love me, and most of all to you. I'm glad that you can help me be worthy of trust—to live up to what you want me to be.

Dear Girlfriend,
I'm having to learn something—that death is a part of life. It's never
fun to talk about, but eventually we'll all have to face it. Maybe
you've already lost someone close to you, someone you love?
Although death feels like the end, it's also a beginning. The great
thing about knowing and loving Jesus is that we'll be able to spend
eternity in Heaven. And that's something to talk about. . . .

A Forever Love

❀ Recipe du Jour ❀

Their newspaper was lying on the front step when the Williams
family returned home from a weekend away. As Jamie
glanced at the headlines, she read:

LOCAL GIRL KILLED

Below the large type was a picture of a girl she knew
well. A tight feeling closed around Jamie's stomach. Sitting
down quickly, she read the article. Then, still unable to really
grasp the news, she looked up.

"Oh, Mom, she died," Jamie moaned. Her voice seemed to
come from a distance. "I can't believe it. Susan died."

Her mom knelt and put her arms around her. "What
happened?"

"She was swimming in front of their cabin and a speed-
boat came too close," answered Jamie.

Sooner or later all of us face the reality of death. Sometimes death becomes a reality because a pet that we love dies suddenly. Sometimes it's a grandparent, parent, brother, sister, or close friend. No matter what the circumstances are, death usually forces us to ask questions like, "What is it like to die?" or "What is Heaven like?"

It helps to know all we can about Heaven. While living on Earth, Jesus told his disciples, "I am going to prepare a place for you . . . so that you will always be with me where I am" (John 14:2, 3 *NLT*). As a result, we know that Heaven is not a city full of strangers. Instead, it's a place where we'll find the best love possible, and Jesus will be there to welcome us.

"Everything I've heard about Heaven makes it sound as though we'll be happy there," said Alyssa. She's right. Death is an experience in which God holds us by the hand, bringing us to a home where we will know joy. We don't know all of the details, but we do know that everything necessary for our happiness will be there.

We might also wonder, *What happens to our bodies?* In 1 Corinthians 15, Paul compares death to the planting of a seed. When we put a seed into the ground, it doesn't grow into a plant unless it "dies" first. The coating around the seed

> Sooner or later all of us face the reality of death.

> Death is an experience in which God holds us by the hand, bringing us to a home where we will know joy.

breaks apart so that the inside of the seed can get nutrients from the soil.

Those of us who like to watch things grow know what happens next. After rain and sunshine, we go outside and see the first green shoots breaking through the brown earth. Soon the tiny shoots unfurl their leaves and grow into delicious veggies or colorful flowers.

Those plants are like what our heavenly bodies will be—beautiful and full of strength. When people are sick or badly hurt, they shed weakness and pain through death, as if the seed coat were splitting apart. Their new bodies are special ones. Paul says they will be full of strength and glory. What's more, those bodies will live forever.

> Those plants are like what our heavenly bodies will be—beautiful and full of strength.

Yet the most important thing to know about death is whether we are ready to face it. As one person put it, "Only if we know how to live are we ready to die."

> The most important thing to know about death is whether we are ready to face it.

Part of knowing how to live is being able to answer these questions: "Do I believe that Jesus died to save me from my sins?" "Have I asked him to forgive my sins?" and "Have I accepted him as my Savior and Lord of my life?"

When we obey Jesus, we receive salvation. We are able to live our lives in such a way that we can face death in the same way that 14-year-old Becky Boyer did. Shortly before she

Burnt Cookies

drowned, Becky wrote this prayer telling about her personal faith in Christ:

Dear Lord,

How beautiful you are to me now! Your radiance fills my heart with joy and gladness. How wonderful it is to sit here and praise your name! I love to read your Word, I love to pray to you, but mostly I love you. My heart is singing alleluia because I know you. First you made me feel happy and joyous; then you helped me commit every part of me to you. You have also filled me with a beautiful power to witness to someone you love so dearly. I know how much you love me and I cannot express to any human person how I feel—only you can understand my joy because you have given it to me. I feel so happy that I'm just going to rest and think of heavenly things. I love you. I honestly love you.

For Becky, dying was a matter of going to see a close friend whom she loved very much.

❀ Main Ingredient ❀

"I am convinced that nothing can ever separate us from his love. Death can't, and life can't." Romans 8:38 *(NLT)*

❀ Temperature Control ❀

Thank you, Lord, that you made it possible for me to believe in you and your resurrection. Thank you for promising that nothing will ever separate me from your love—that you, my very best friend, will always be with me.

Dear Girlfriend,
Have you ever been so angry, you thought you'd explode? Maybe it
was your mom or dad, or a younger sibling or friend who pushed
you to the limit. For me anger can be tough to deal with. Often it
sneaks up on me when I least expect it. Before I know it, I'm out of
control, saying and doing things I regret. But I'm glad about one
thing. There's hope! With some hard work and a lot of help from
God, we can tame the anger monster within. . . .

Monster Dog vs. Wonder Pup

❀ Recipe du Jour ❀

With an angry snarl, the big dog jumped up on Katie, his paws
knocked her backward. Frightened, she began to edge away.
Then she was overwhelmed with relief when the owner
grabbed the dog's collar.

Most of us are like Katie—afraid of a dog whose temper
flares unexpectedly. *Will I be hurt?* we wonder. We would just
as soon keep our distance. We'd rather play with a fun-loving
puppy whose personality we can trust—one who greets us, tail
wagging and eager to play.

But, sometimes, even a dog has a right to be angry.
"Hey!" called Tina. From the hallway she'd heard their cocker
spaniel growl. Dashing into the kitchen, she picked up her 2
-year-old brother. "No! No!" she told him. "You can't pull a
dog's tail while he's eating."

Burnt Cookies

Like Tina, we have a right, even a responsibility, to be angry when we see wrong things being done. Jesus was angry when he overturned the tables of the moneychangers in the temple. He didn't want to see people using his Father's house in the wrong way.

> We have a right, even a responsibility, to be angry when we see wrong things being done.

Jordan offered her own example: "It makes me mad when I see people trashing the environment."

"Yeah, or when a bully picks on a smaller kid," Ali chimed in.

But most of the time when we're angry, it's not over things that need to be fixed. More often we're blowing things out of proportion and letting them get to us. Perhaps we've hurt people that way. Maybe they've withdrawn from us, hiding their feelings because of something we've said.

"Usually I spout off at someone and then feel bad about it later," said one girl. "I want to be the kind of person others like to be around. But what can I do about it?"

> I want to be the kind of person others like to be around. But what can I do about it?

Believe it or not, it's easier to be thoughtful of others when we're able to get enough sleep. Right now our bodies may be changing so fast that it's hard to get as much rest as we need. Sometimes our brains feel like eggs dropped on the floor and our eyelids seem coated with sand. Often it takes real effort to get more sleep.

What we eat also plays an important part. Soda, candy, cake, and other sugary foods can make us more irritable. Following a balanced diet has big benefits—eating fruits and veggies even helps our complexions.

We can also try to avoid arguments when we feel especially irritable or out-of-sorts. On days like that, some things may bug us more than they would at other times. If we feel edgy, we can try to think before we act or speak by asking ourselves, *Am I blowing this up? Is it really important?* We might be surprised to learn that we're fighting over something that really doesn't mean that much to us.

Am I blowing this up? Is it really important?

At times it's a good idea to talk to someone before reaching the bursting point. We'll be less likely to explode if we tell the right person our frustrations and worries before they build up too much. "Sometimes I feel like a can of soda," Amber said. "When I talk to someone, it's like popping the top and letting the fizz come out. When someone listens to me, the fizz settles and the pressure is off."

Will we still become irritable or be bugged by our tempers when we're older? Of course! Whether we're 16 or 63. Even when we're trying hard, angry words still might get away from us. How can we go on from there?

That's where forgiveness comes in. Now and then our homework is filled with cross-outs and sloppy handwriting.

Burnt Cookies

Think of those messy spots as times when we lose our tempers or as moments when we're angry and irritable.

Even when we're trying hard, angry words still might get away from us.

When we say, "I'm sorry," God reaches down with his giant eraser. He erases our sins so that we can start over with a clean sheet of paper. When we receive God's forgiveness, we also can ask for the joy and peace of his Spirit. We can be as happy as a friendly puppy—giving love to those around us.

❀ Main Ingredient ❀

"'Don't sin by letting anger gain control over you. Don't let the sun go down while you are still angry.'" Ephesians 4:26 (NLT)

❀ Temperature Control ❀

Help me, Lord, to speak up against the things I should be angry about. But forgive me for the times when I am cranky or lose my temper. Fill me with your Spirit's presence. Let your joy and peace flow through me to others.

Paging Mr. Wonderful

❀ Recipe du Jour ❀

Annie's face shone. Her quick smile lit even the depths of her deep brown eyes. She was having so much fun at the party!

All of us look forward to parties. Our enthusiasm bubbles up just thinking about them. When they're over, we talk about them with our friends, sometimes for several days. As we go to parties or do things with small groups or families, most of us have only fun in mind. This is a special time in our lives—and we like the excitement that being with others can bring.

Yet while we're having fun, we can also learn about other people, and boys in particular. We can look for certain qualities and decide what we value most in the people we'd like to have for our best friends. If there's a boy we especially like, we can enjoy finding out more about him. One thing we'll want to know is if he builds people up or pushes them down.

"Most of the time I think he's great," said one girl about a boy in her class. "Yet every once in a while he starts throwing around sarcastic remarks. You know, things meant to be funny. But he goes too far and hurts other people."

There's a fine line where sarcasm loses its humor and begins to bite. Usually we prefer being around someone who is thoughtful about the feelings of others. It's a quality that goes deep and wears well with time.

Justin is that kind of person. One day as he pedaled down the street, he noticed his 5-year-old neighbor boy having trouble learning to ride his new bike.

"Hey, Trevor!" he called. "Want some help?" Justin left his own bike and steadied Trevor's until he was able to take off on his own.

As we think about friendships, we should also know how a boy looks at life. Is he always pushing the limits? Or does he support the rules that are important to everyone?

One night Nate took Katie's older sister Christy to see a movie. Later Christy told Katie about it. On the way home, Nate had car trouble and had to pull over to the side of the road.

"Uh-oh," he groaned. "I'm not going to be able to get you home on time. Your parents will be upset, won't they?"

Christy nodded, biting her lip.

Nate sighed. "OK, let's think what to do. I don't want to leave you alone, so let's call for help." Using Christy's cell phone, he found a service station that was open, then said, "I'll call your parents and explain what happened."

It takes courage to meet a hard situation head-on like Nate did. As time goes on, he'll handle other things in much the same way. For good or for bad, a person's future is shaped by the way he handles things now.

As we get to know boys, we need to find out what they believe about Christ. The spiritual side of a person's life shapes everything else he does. Our friendships can include those who aren't Christians so that we can share Christ with them. Yet it's important to choose our closest friends from among those who believe in Christ with the same level of commitment that we have.

As we get to know boys, we need to find out what they believe about Christ.

We can avoid much unhappiness by choosing friends—especially the boys we date—who are strongly committed Christians. In time this will help us, because the person we will marry someday will be a guy we've dated. "I'm not leaving my husband up to chance," said Jennifer. "I'm praying about him now. I want to marry someone who will help me grow closer to Jesus. I don't want to be with someone who stands in the way of my relationship with Jesus."

The spiritual side of a person's life shapes everything else he does.

As Christian girls we can begin now to ask, "Lord, guide my friendships with boys. When it's time to get serious with someone, I want him to be your choice for me."

What will happen as a result? Our common sense and spiritual wisdom will help us recognize the qualities needed for a heartwarming lifelong relationship. And God will help us see what's important about the boys with whom we become acquainted. So let's keep our eyes open for whatever God wants to give.

❀ Main Ingredient ❀

"Above all else, guard your heart, for it affects everything you do." Proverbs 4:23 *(NLT)*

❀ Temperature Control ❀

Lord, I ask you to guide me in my friendships. Wherever I am—at church, school, or small groups—help me to see the qualities in a boy that are important for me to recognize. When it's time for me to choose a Mr. Wonderful, show me your choice for me.

Stored for Safekeeping

✿ Recipe du Jour ✿

Kylee kicked off her shoes and lay back in the soft grass on a
bank high above the river. Overhead, the red-orange leaves
of an oak tree rustled in the breeze. Beyond that, clouds raced
across an autumn sky.

For an instant Kylee wondered what it would be like to live
where it was warm all year long. Soon the cold winds of winter would keep her from coming to this spot.

Not far away, other kids roasted hot dogs around a campfire. But for just this moment Kylee wanted to be alone. To
make time stand still and think about what was happening in

her life. To store the memory of this special place for safe-keeping. To think about God and all that he meant to her.

Upstream, a swirl of golden elm leaves blew into the water. Sitting up again, Kylee leaned forward and looked down into the river. The leaves dipped and bobbed in the swirling current, floating like tiny canoes to some far-off land.

"Thanks, God," Kylee whispered. "Thanks for this memory."

What other memories has God given me? she asked herself. *What ideas have I stored in my mind to make me strong?*

Watching the golden leaves drift downstream, Kylee began naming memories to herself.

What ideas have I stored in my mind to make me strong?

Love, she thought. Love I don't deserve. Love that is given to me anyway. Love from God and love from my family.

Loyalty. Mom and Dad sticking by me even when I do something wrong—forgiving me the way God does.

Freedom. Freedom to think. To be myself. To make wise choices. Freedom to be responsible to others who bring good into my life.

Fun. Good times with friends. Roasting marshmallows over a campfire. Sharing stories, singing, and laughing. Sleepovers with friends. A weekend like this at a church camp.

The feel of summer as I race for the lake. Flipping onto my back to float in sunlit water.

The winter wind stinging my cheeks out on the slopes. New powder. Snow swirling upward past my snowboard.

The snap of a ball in my hands. The surprise of cheers filling the gym.

And knowledge? Some of it hard-earned. But there when I need it. *And what else, Lord?*

The tear on my mother's cheek, quickly wiped away when I brought her a breakfast tray on Mother's Day.

The good feeling I had when I cleaned everything out from under my bed without anyone saying I must.

An unexpected smile from the boy I hope will like me.

The baby squirrel I found whimpering in a window-well. Feeding it with an eyedropper filled with milk. Carrying the squirrel in the hood of my sweatshirt until it climbed a tree on its own.

Kylee smiled. Good memories. Memories that made her strong. *Thanks, God.*

But then she wondered. *What else have I stored in my mind?*

The hard times. When she was sick, or someone she loved was sick. When she was scared, really scared. Or unhappy. Miserable, in fact.

Walking down a hallway when she was new at school. Learning that her grandpa had an accident. Nearly failing a test, even though she had studied.

What was there about those times? Could she say thank you, not because those times were hard, but for some other reason? What did she remember about those times? What had she learned about God that no one could take from her?

You were with me, God. You were my best friend.

Then Kylee knew. *You were with me, God. You were my best friend. I hung onto the Bible promises you gave me. I repeated them to myself, and I knew that you were with me, even though I couldn't see you.*

Suddenly tears welled up in Kylee's eyes. *You were listening, even when I couldn't see answers to prayer. You were with me when everything seemed hard, so hard that I couldn't handle it. Wherever I was, every moment of the day or night, no matter what was happening, you were with me.*

You were faithful. I can trust you. Not only have you died on the cross to give me salvation and eternal life, you have given me the ability to live now!

Could she say thank you, not because those times were hard, but for some other reason?

And then Kylee wondered, *What about my future?*

What about the ice of winter when she could no longer see golden leaves swirling downstream, reminding her how to be thankful? What would happen when she grew a year or two older and everything changed? What had she stored in her mind for that time?

In that moment Kylee knew that whatever winds came,

she wanted one thing. To live in such a way that she let nothing take away her relationship with the Lord. She wouldn't let anything spoil her belief that, if she allowed him, God would be with her in everything.

From deep in her memory the promise came. "'For I know the plans I have for you,' says the LORD. 'They are plans for good and not for disaster, to give you a future and a hope'" (Jeremiah 29:11, *NLT*).

> "'For I know the plans I have for you,' says the Lord. 'They are plans for good and not disaster, to give you a future and a hope.'"

With the promise stored in her mind, Kylee stood up. With the memory of that verse where no one could take it from her, she took one last look at the river. There with the elm leaves floating downstream like tiny canoes, she prayed. *Thank you, Lord. Thank for promising to be with me always.*

❀ Main Ingredient ❀

God said, "'In those days when you pray, I will listen. If you look for me in earnest, you will find me when you seek me.'" Jeremiah 29:12, 13 *(NLT)*

❀ Temperature Control ❀

Thank you, Lord, for the yesterdays and the todays. Thank you that you're a loving and faithful God who promises always to be with me. And thank you for all that you're going to do with my life.

Here's what I think...

Dear Girlfriend,
Do you think very much about the future? You know, dream about
what you'll do, where you'll live, who will be part of your life? With
all my heart, I believe God has some great things in store for both
of us. I feel sure that he wants to be part of our tomorrows. But I
wonder, should we start preparing for our tomorrows today? . . .

Dream On

❋ Recipe du Jour ❋

Do you ever dream about being the most popular girl in school? Or being someone so successful that the whole world knows about you? At one time or another, most of us think it would be fun to be famous. But popularity, success, and fame don't come easily.

Elise's first book was selling well and her second had just been published. When she attended a writers' conference she met a well-known author who said, "You have a good deal of ability. I've known great writers and you will be one of them."

Full of gratitude for his kind words, Elise smiled and thanked him. *That's just the encouragement I need,* she thought.

Still feeling excited, she returned home and tried to return to her writing. But the flow of words that she normally produced had slowed to a trickle. She could have hung a sign on her PC that said, **CRASHED! USELESS! NO GOOD!**

After a week of frustration, Elise sat back and asked herself, *What's wrong here?*

As she thought about it, she realized that she had mixed up the order of things. *Here I am,* Elise told herself, *focusing on being great instead of on what I need to say. I'm thinking so much about being a great writer that I can't write a single sentence. Nothing seems good enough to count as great writing!*

It took a while before Elise's computer raced along with its usual ease. The flow of words came back only after she was honest with herself. *What is success?* she wondered. *Is it wealth or fame?*

Success is doing well whatever job is right in front of me.

She decided it wasn't either of those things. Wanting to stay on target, Elise printed some words on a large piece of paper and propped it up on her desk: "Success is doing well whatever job is right in front of me."

A girl named Lyn Crosby put it another way:

> "The pieces of the puzzle
> that make up my today
> are pieces of tomorrow
> as well as yesterday."

When we work on a jigsaw puzzle, we put together one

small area, then another. Gradually we fit those sections together until the entire pattern takes shape. Right now, in the puzzle of our lives we can't see the whole pattern. Yet we can ask, "What pieces of tomorrow am I holding in my hands today?"

What pieces of tomorrow am I holding in my hands today?

To find some of those pieces we need to decide, "What is really important to me? What is my goal for the future?"

We also can ask God, "Lord, what do you want me to be?" We have the privilege of asking him to show us what he wants for our lives. It's fun to know that, if God calls us to do something, he will give us the ability to do it.

Then let's think about the words beneath a window in the Library of Congress: "Too low they build who build beneath the stars."

When we belong to God, we have the privilege of dreaming big—as big as the potential he gives each one of us. He wants us to "shine like stars in the universe" (Philippians 2:15, *NIV*).

When we belong to God, we have the privilege of dreaming big. He wants us to shine like stars in the universe.

If we pray and ask for his leading, he will set a dream in our hearts—the desire to be the people he wants us to be, to work toward that goal which he gives us. If the dream is his, he will help us shape our potential into something worthwhile and beautiful. When we keep our gaze on him, our path

Burnt Cookies

toward reaching that dream won't be filled with striving after the wrong thing.

Instead, our lives will be marked by his timing, his help, and his blessing.

Sometimes we make the mistake of thinking that physical beauty would be our most valuable asset. But, think about this sign taped to Jenny's mirror:

**NOT EVERYONE CAN BE PRETTY,
BUT EVERYONE CAN BE BEAUTIFUL.**

"Beautiful! Not me!" you might mutter, having only the image of a TV star in your mind.

Yet, we need to remember that we are not drawn to Christ because of his physical appearance. We are drawn to him because of who he was and how he died for us. We honor Jesus because he rose up from the dead to live for us forever. We worship him because of who he was while on Earth and because of who he continues to be. His love and kindness toward all of us make him a beautiful person.

Whatever we do, God wants to be the most important part of our lives.

No matter what dream is part of our puzzles—whether it's being a homemaker, exploring the depths of the ocean or the heights of space, becoming a teacher, doctor, or animal trainer—it's possible to dream big. God may help us build a home where love is present. Or he may help us concentrate on a career. Or he may help us creatively do both. But whatever we do, God wants to be the most important part of our lives.

Jesus, our Savior and friend, wants to have a living, vital role, not only in our todays, but also in our tomorrows. And so, as we build our lives, we can pray, "Lord, I want to help others. I give all my abilities to you. Show me how to develop the gifts you have given me in a way that honors you."

As singer Jane Henley said, "Success is allowing God to use the ability he has given me." Another wise person summed it up: "What you are is God's gift to you. What you become is your gift to God."

What are the pieces of your tomorrow?

Dream on, Girlfriend. And know something really big. Whatever your future holds, your very best friend is Jesus.

❀ Main Ingredient ❀

"Now glory be to God! By his mighty power at work within us, he is able to accomplish infinitely more than we would ever dare to ask or hope." Ephesians 3:20 (NLT)

❀ Temperature Control ❀

Lord, I want you to have the most important part in the puzzle of my tomorrows. Help me to use my abilities according to your plan for my life.

Here's what I think...

Dear Girlfriend,
Here's a quick guide to help you find what you're looking for when you need it the most!

OVERCOMING FEAR

"I can do everything with the help of Christ who gives me the strength I need." Philippians 4:13 *(NLT)*
—*Fear Factor, 8*

SELF-IMAGE

"My gracious favor is all you need. My power works best in your weakness." 2 Corinthians 12:9 *(NLT)*
—*Target Practice, 12*

TRUSTING GOD

"God has said, 'I will never fail you. I will never forsake you.'" Hebrews 13:5 *(NLT)*
—*Good Night Superstar, 18*

TOUGH LOVE

"Honor your father and mother, as the LORD your God commanded you. Then you will live a long, full life in the land the LORD your God will give you." Deuteronomy 5:16 *(NLT)*
—*Friday Night Freedom, 24*

RESISTING PEER PRESSURE

"Be strong with the Lord's mighty power." Ephesians 6:10 *(NLT)*
—*Contents Under Pressure, 30*

TURNING FAILURE INTO SUCCESS

"And we know that God causes everything to work together for the good of those who love God and are called according to his purpose for them." Romans 8:28 *(NLT)*
—*Burnt Cookies, 34*

EXCELLENCE VS. PERFECTION

"God has given each of us the ability to do certain things well." Romans 12:6 *(NLT)*
—*Breathing Room, 38*

BEING CONTENT

"'Choose today whom you will serve. . . . But as for me and my family, we will serve the Lord.'" Joshua 24:15 *(NLT)*
—*My Good Life, 44*

GETTING ALONG WITH OTHERS

"God saved you by his special favor when you believed. And you can't take credit for this; it is a gift from God." Ephesians 2:8 *(NLT)*
—*War Zone, 50*

Burnt Cookies

MAKING NEW FRIENDS

"There are 'friends' who destroy each other, but a real friend sticks closer than a brother." Proverbs 18:24 *(NLT)*
—*Sole Survivor, 56*

DEALING WITH DIVORCE

"Don't worry about anything; instead, pray about everything. Tell God what you need, and thank him for all he has done." Philippians 4:6 *((NLT)*
—*Splitsville, 62*

BUILDING TRUST WITH PARENTS

"Those who obey God's word really do love him. That is the way to know whether or not we live in him. Those who say they live in God should live their lives as Christ did." 1 John 2:5, 6 *(NLT)*
—*Olympic Gold!, 66*

DEALING WITH DEATH

"I am convinced that nothing can ever separate us from his love. Death can't, and life can't." Romans 8:38 *(NLT)*
—*A Forever Love, 70*

ANGER MANAGEMENT

"Don't sin by letting anger gain control over you. Don't let the sun go down while you are still angry." Ephesians 4:26 *(NLT)*
—*Monster Dog vs. Wonder Pup, 74*

DATING

"Above all else, guard your heart, for it affects everything you do." Proverbs 4:23 *(NLT)*
—*Paging Mr. Wonderful, 78*

GOD'S FAITHFULNESS

God said, "In those days when you pray I will listen. If you look for me in earnest, you will find me when you seek me." Jeremiah 29:12,13 *(NLT)*
—*Stored for Safekeeping, 82*

GOALS AND DREAMS

"Now glory be to God! By his mighty power at work within us, he is able to accomplish infinitely more than we would ever dare to ask or hope." Ephesians 3:20 *(NLT)*
—*Dream On, 88*

Cool books for preteens!

DEAR GOD,
LET'S TALK ABOUT YOU
0-7847-1247-6

HI GOD,
LET'S TALK ABOUT MY LIFE
0-7847-1246-8

These devotional journals will help you face everyday issues
and answer common questions about God
with devotions, biblical advice, and prayer starters.

BELIEVE IT!
0-7847-1393-6

Through incredible, readable rhymes,
you'll discover answers to mind-blowing questions about
God and the Bible.